Summer Collection
for Keyboard

Music arranged and processed by Barnes Music Engraving Ltd
East Sussex TN22 4HA, UK

Cover design by xheight Limited

Published 1996

BEACH BABY

Words and Music by John Carter and Gill Shakespeare

Suggested Registration: Saxophone
Rhythm: Shuffle
Tempo: ♩ = 120

Do you re-mem-ber back in old L. A. __ oh, __ oh, when ev-ery-bo-dy drove a

Chev-ro-let, __ oh, __ oh? What-ev-er hap-pened to the boy next door, the

sun-tanned crew-cut All A-me-ri-can Male? Re-mem-ber danc-ing at the

high school hop __ oh, __ oh, the dress I ru-ined with the so-da pop, __ oh __ oh?

I did-n't re-cog-nise the girl next door, __ the beat-up sneak-ers, and the

po-ny tail. __ Beach ba-by, beach ba-by,

give me your hand, give me some-thing that I___ can re-mem-ber,_____

just like be-fore,_ we could walk___ by the shore_ in the moon-light._____

Beach ba-by, beach ba-by, there on the sand, from Ju-ly_

__ to the end__ of Sep-tem-ber,_____ surf-ing was fun,_ we'd be out

__ in the sun ev-ery day._____

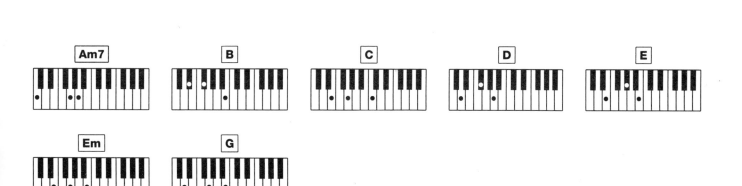

THE BOYS OF SUMMER

Words and Music by Don Henley and Mike Campbell

Suggested Registration: Piano
Rhythm: 8 Beat
Tempo: ♩ = 168

No-bo-dy on the road,　　no-bo-dy on the beach,

I feel it in the air,　　the sum-mer's out of reach.

Emp - ty lake,＿　emp - ty streets,　the sun goes down a - lone.＿

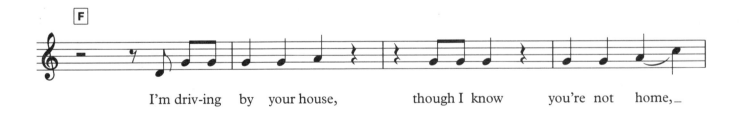

I'm driv-ing by your house,　　though I know you're not home,＿

but I can see you,＿　your brown skin shin-in' in the sun,

you got your hair combed back, and your sun-glass-es on, ba - by,

and I can tell you, my love for you__ will still be strong,

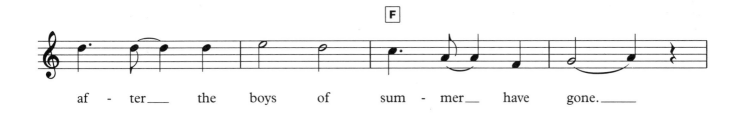

af - ter__ the boys of sum - mer__ have gone.__

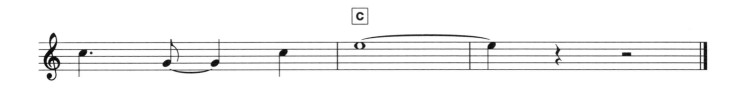

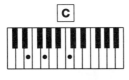
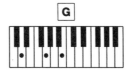
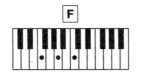

Bring Me Sunshine

Words by Sylvia Dee / Music by Arthur Kent

Suggested Registration: Vibraphone
Rhythm: Swing
Tempo: ♩ = 176

Bring me sun - shine ___ in your smile, ___

bring me laugh - ter ___ all the while. ___

In this world where we live there should be more hap - pi - ness,

___ so much joy you can give to each brand new bright to - mor -

- row. Make me hap - py ___ through the years, ___

ne - ver bring me___ a - ny tears.___

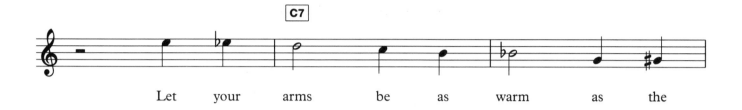

Let your arms be as warm as the

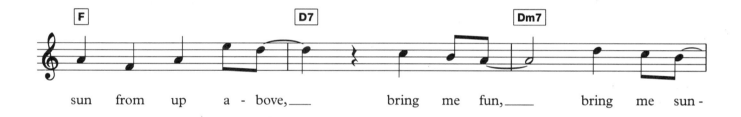

sun from up a - bove,___ bring me fun,___ bring me sun -

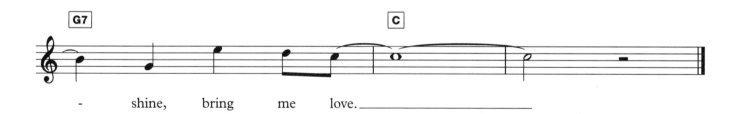

- shine, bring me love._____

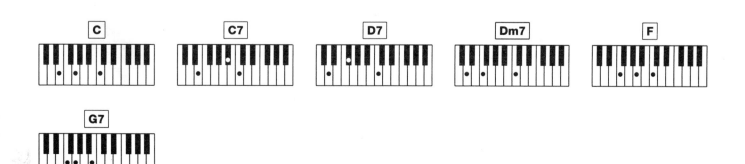

Eviva España

Words by Leo Rozenstraeten / Music by Leo Caerts

Suggested Registration: Acoustic Guitar
Rhythm: March
Tempo: ♩ = 120

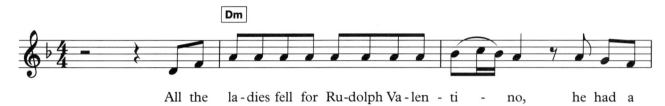

All the la-dies fell for Ru-dolph Va-len-ti - no, he had a

bea-no back in those bal-my days. He knew ev-ery time you meet an i - cy

crea - ture, you've got to teach her hot blood-ed la-tin ways, but

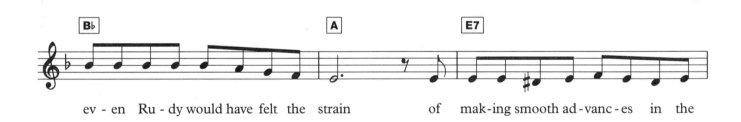

ev - en Ru-dy would have felt the strain of mak-ing smooth ad-vanc-es in the

rain. Oh, this year I'm off to sun-ny Spain, e -

THE GIRL FROM IPANEMA
(GAROTA DE IPANEMA)

Original words by Vinicius de Moraes / English words by Norman Gimbel / Music by Antonio Carlos Jobim

Suggested Registration: Flute
Rhythm: Bossa Nova
Tempo: ♩ = 116

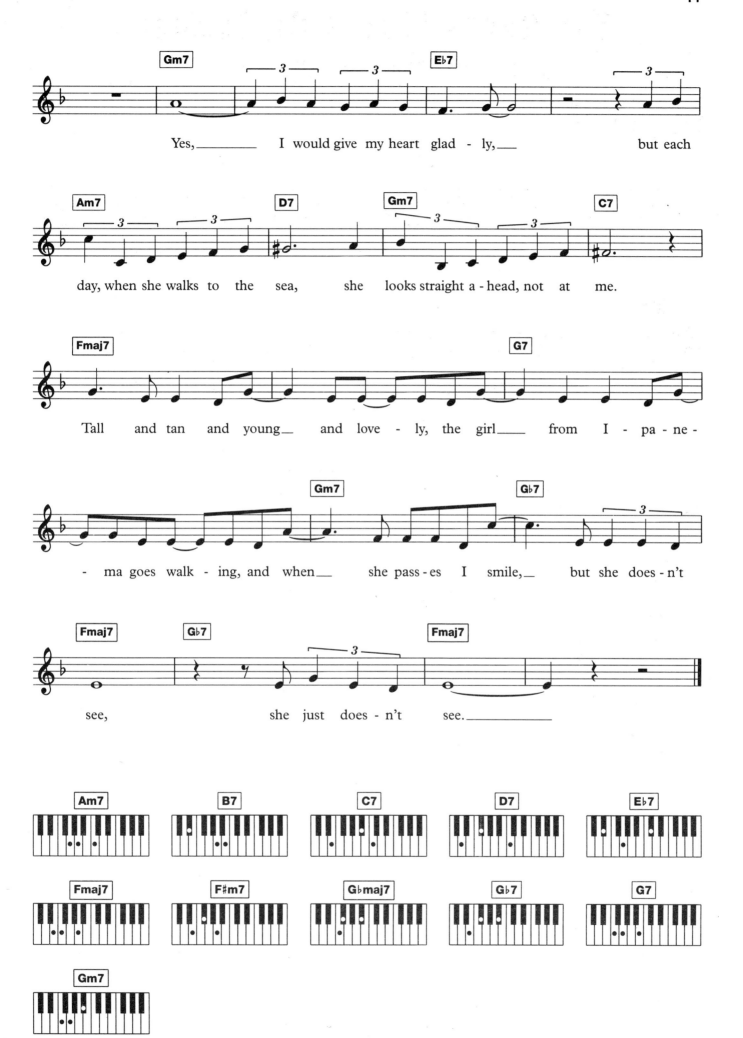

The Green Leaves Of Summer

Words by Paul Francis Webster / Music by Dimitri Tiomkin

Suggested Registration: Oboe
Rhythm: Slow Rock 6/8
Tempo: ♩. = 60

Groovin'

Words and Music by Felix Cavaliere and Eddie Brigatti Jnr

Suggested Registration: Harmonica
Rhythm: Slow Rhumba
Tempo: ♩ = 100

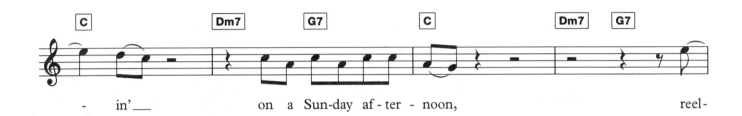

Groov-

in'___ on a Sun-day af-ter-noon, reel-

-in',___ could-n't get a-way too soon.

I can't i-ma-gine a-ny - thing that's bet - ter,___ the world is ours when-ev - er

we're to-ge-ther,___ there' ain't a place I like to be in-stead of___ groov-

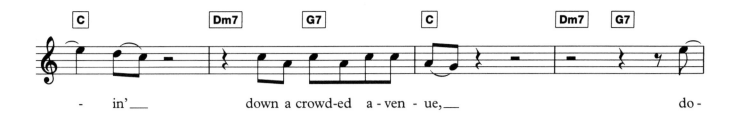

- in'____   down a crowd-ed a - ven - ue,___   do -

- in'____   a - ny-thing we like to   do.___

There's al-ways lots of things that   we can see,_____   we could be a - ny-where we

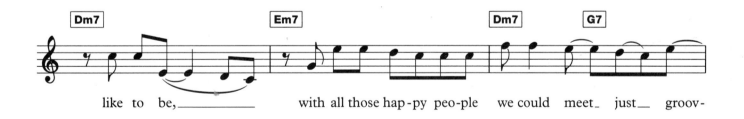

like to be,_____   with all those hap-py peo-ple   we could meet_ just_ groov-

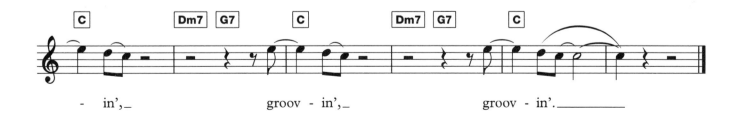

- in',_   groov - in',_   groov - in'._____

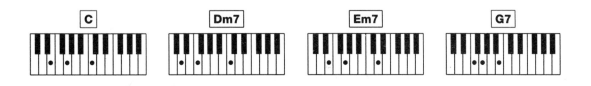

I Do Like To Be Beside The Seaside

Words and Music by John A Glover-Kind

Suggested Registration: Electric Organ
Rhythm: March 6/8
Tempo: ♩. = 120

Oh! I do like to be be - side the sea - side,

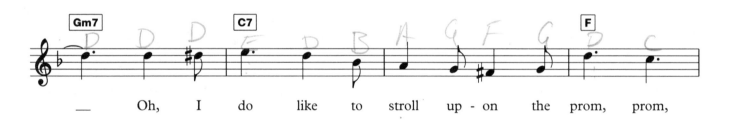

— I do like to be be - side the sea.

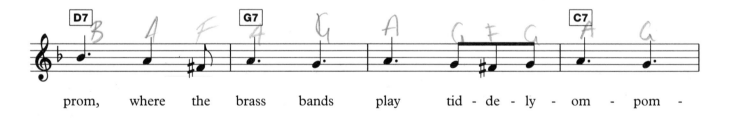

— Oh, I do like to stroll up - on the prom, prom,

prom, where the brass bands play tid - de - ly - om - pom -

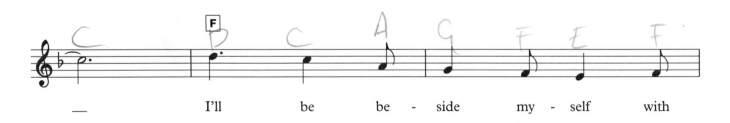

- pom. So, just let me be be - side the sea - side,

— I'll be be - side my - self with

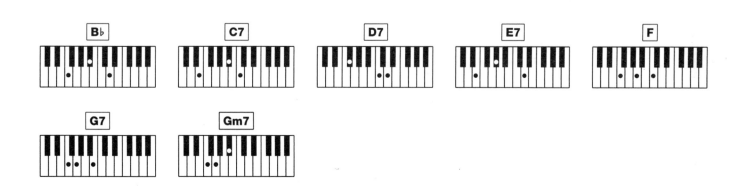

I Get Around

Words and Music by Brian Wilson

Suggested Registration: Electric Guitar
Rhythm: Rock
Tempo: ♩ = 132

Round, round, get a-round, I get a-round, get a-round, round, round,

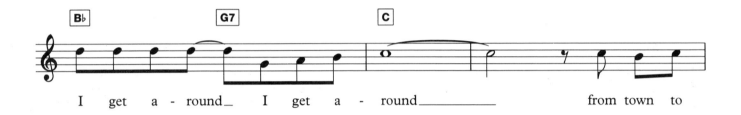

I get a-round_ I get a-round_____ from town to

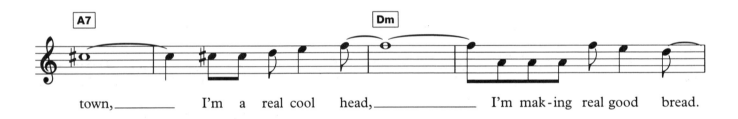

town,_____ I'm a real cool head,_____ I'm mak-ing real good bread.

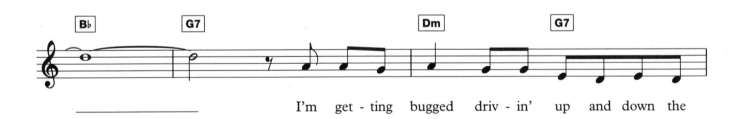

_____ I'm get-ting bugged driv-in' up and down the

same ol' strip,_ I got-ta find a new place where the kids are hip._

In The Summertime

Words and Music by Ray Dorset

Suggested Registration: Banjo
Rhythm: Bluegrass / Country
Tempo: ♩ = 84

In the sum-mer - time when the wea-ther is high, _ you can

stretch right up, an' _ touch _ the sky. _ When the wea-ther's fine, you got

wo - men, you got wo - men on your mind. Have a

drink, have a drive, go out and see what you can find. If her

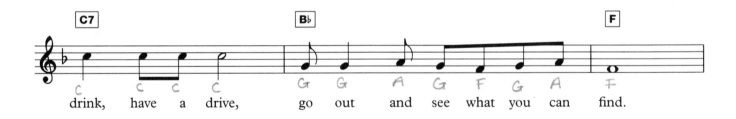

If her dad-die's rich, take her out for a meal, _ if her

dad - die's poor, just _ do as you feel, _ speed a - long the lane, do a

ton,___ or a ton and twen-ty five. When the

sun goes down, you can make it, make it good in a lay-by.

We're not grey peo-ple, we're not dir-ty, we're not mean, we love

ev-ery-bo - dy, but we do as we please. When the wea-ther's fine, we go

fish-ing or go swim-ming in the sea. We're al-ways hap-py, life's for

liv-ing yeah! That's our phi-lo-so-phy._____

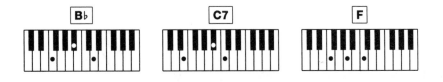

La Isla Bonita

Words and Music by Madonna Ciccone, Pat Leonard and Bruce Geitch

Suggested Registration: Steel Drum
Rhythm: Samba / Latin
Tempo: ♩ = 100

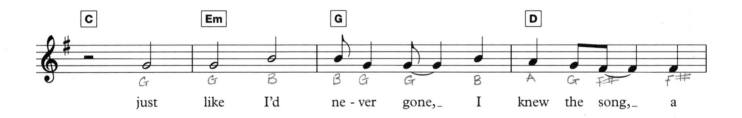

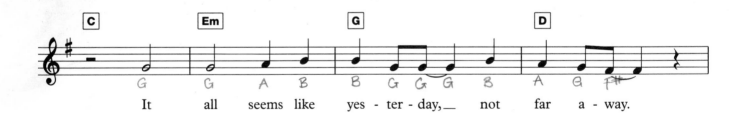

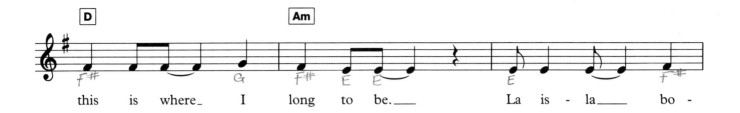

this is where I long to be. La is - la bo -

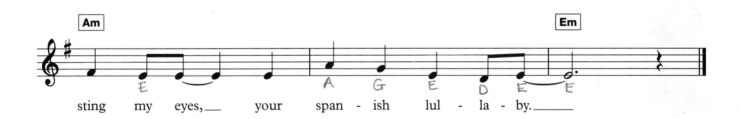

- ni - ta, and when the sam - ba played,

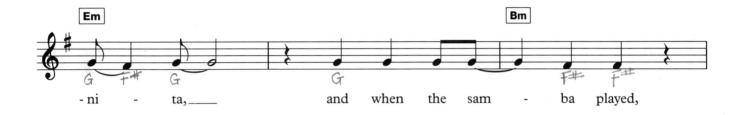

the sun would set so high, ring through my ears, and

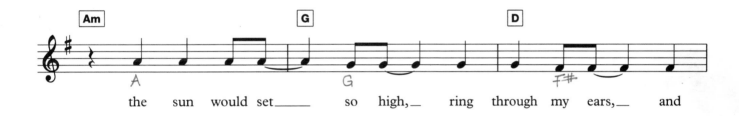

sting my eyes, your span - ish lul - la - by.

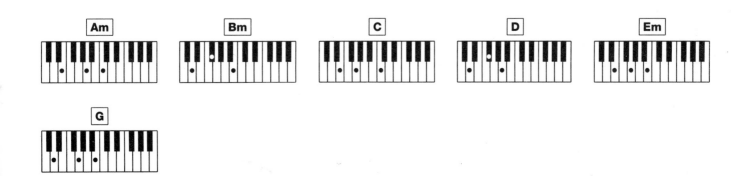

Let's Twist Again

Words and Music by Kal Mann and Dave Appell

Suggested Registration: Saxophone
Rhythm: 8 Beat / Rock 'n' Roll
Tempo: ♩ = 152

Let's twist a - gain, __ like we did last sum - mer, __ yeah, let's twist a - gain, __ like we did last year. Don't - cha re - mem - ber when __ things were real - ly hum - min' __ yeah, let's twist a - gain, __ twist - in' time is here. An' round, an' round an'

up an' down we go a - gain,____ oh,

ba - by, make me know you love me so a - gain.

____ Let's twist a - gain,____ like we did last

sum - mer,____ yeah, let's twist a - gain,____

like we did last year._____

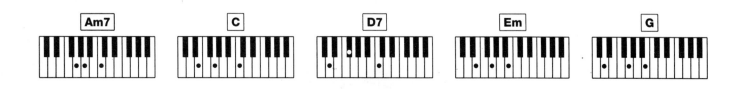

A Summer Place

By Max Steiner

Suggested Registration: Strings
Rhythm: Slow Rock 6/8
Tempo: ♩. = 56

Summer Of '69

Words and Music by Bryan Adams and Jim Vallance

Suggested Registration: Electric Guitar
Rhythm: Rock
Tempo: ♩ = 138

I got my first real six - string, bought it at the five and dime,

played it till my fin - gers_ bled, was the sum-mer of 'six - ty nine.

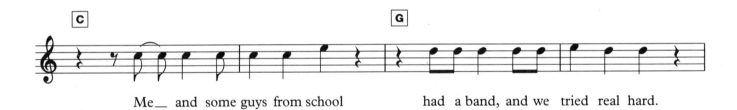

Me_ and some guys from school had a band, and we tried real hard.

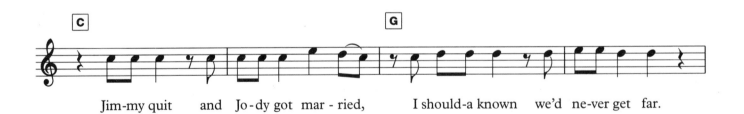

Jim-my quit and Jo-dy got mar - ried, I should-a known we'd ne-ver get far.

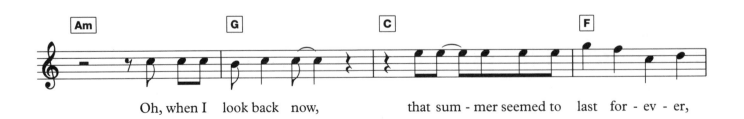

Oh, when I look back now, that sum - mer seemed to last for - ev - er,

and_ if I had the choice, yeah, I'd al-ways wan - na be there,

those were the best days of my__ life, back in the sum-mer of

'six - ty nine, back in the sum-mer of 'six - ty nine.

Those were the best days of my__ life._____

Summer (The First Time)

Words and Music by Bobby Goldsboro

Suggested Registration: Piano
Rhythm: Soft Rock
Tempo: ♩ = 84

Was a hot af-ter-noon,   the last day in June,_   and the

sun was a de-mon.   The clouds were a-fraid,   of-

-ten in the shade,   and the pave-ment was steam-in'.   I

told Bil-ly Ray_   in his red Chev-ro-let,_   need-ed time for some think-in'.

I was just walk-in' by_   when I looked in her eye,_   and I

swore it was wink-in'.   When she looked at me   I heard her

soft - ly say, 'I know you're young, you don't know what to do or say, but

stay with me un - ti the sun has gone a - way, and I will chase the boy in you a -

- way. Was a hot af - ter - noon, the

last day in June,_ and the sun was a de - mon.

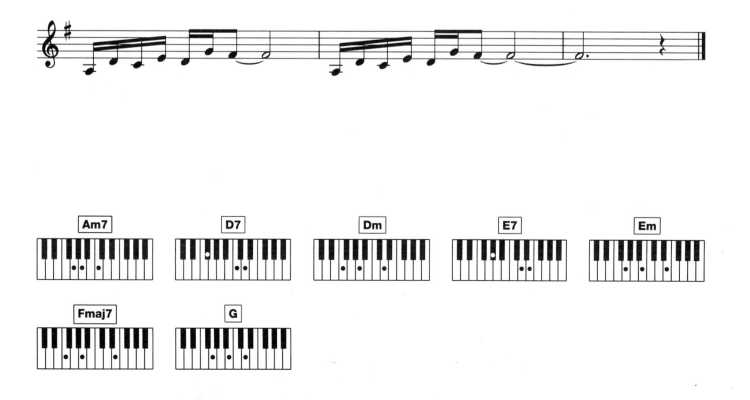

Summer Wind

German Words by Hans Bradtke / English Words by Johnny Mercer / Music by Henry Mayer

Suggested Registration: Vibraphone
Rhythm: Medium Swing
Tempo: ♩ = 100

The sum-mer wind came blow-in' in a - cross the sea, __

it ling-ered there to touch your hair, and walk with me. __

All sum-mer long we sang a song, and strolled the gold - en

sand. Two sweet - hearts and the sum - mer wind,

like paint-ed kites the days and nights went fly - ing by. __

Warner Chappell Music Ltd, London W1Y 3FA

The world was new be-neath a blue um-brel-la sky,__

then soft-er than a pi-per man, one

day it called to you, I lost you to the

sum-mer wind, the sum-mer wind._____

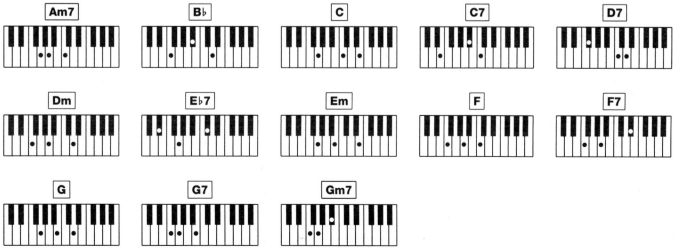

Summertime

By George Gershwin, Dubose and Dorothy Heyward and Ira Gershwin

Suggested Registration: Harmonica
Rhythm: Slow Swing
Tempo: ♩ = 76

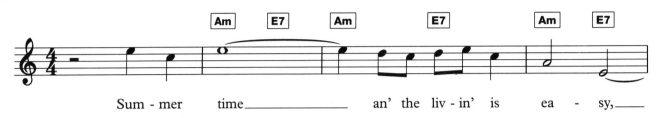

Sum - mer time____ an' the liv-in' is ea - sy,___

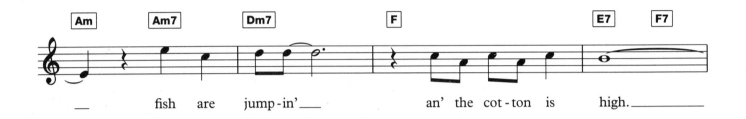

_ fish are jump-in'___ an' the cot-ton is high.___

_ Oh, yo' dad-dy's rich,_ an' yo' ma is good look - in',___

_ so hush lit - tle ba - by don'___ yo' cry.___

_ One of these morn - in's, yo' goin' to rise___ up sing - in',___

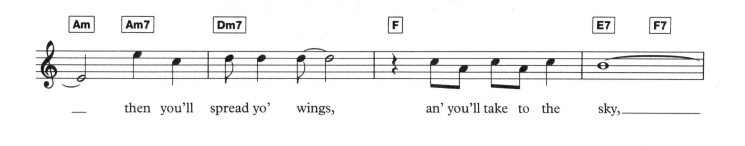

then you'll spread yo' wings, an' you'll take to the sky,_____

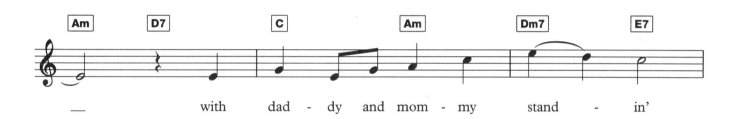

but till that morn-in',___ there's a - no-thin' can harm you,___

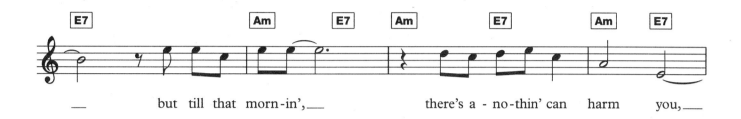

with dad - dy and mom - my stand - in'

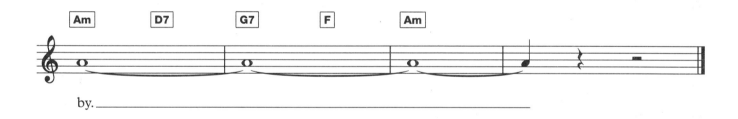

by. _____

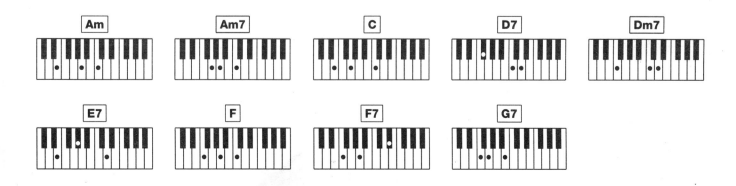

Summertime Blues

Words and Music by Eddie Cochran and Jerry Capehart

Suggested Registration: Electric Guitar
Rhythm: 8 beat
Tempo: ♩ = 144

I'm gon-na take my prob-lem to the U-nit-ed Na-tions.

Well, I called my con-gress-man, and he said, quote, 'I'd like to help you son, but you're too young to vote.'_____ Some-times I won-der what I'm a-gon-na do,___ but there ain't no cure for the sum-mer-time__ blues.

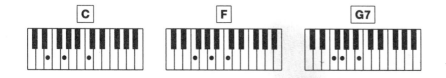

Sunny Afternoon

Words and Music by Ray Davies

Suggested Registration: Clarinet
Rhythm: Pop Swing
Tempo: ♩ = 152

The tax-man's tak-en all my dough, and

left me in my state-ly home,_ laz-ing on a

sun-ny af-ter-noon, and I can't sail my yacht,_ he's

tak-en ev-ery-thing I've got,___ all I've got's this

sun-ny af-ter-noon.

Save me, save me, save me from this squeeze,___

I've got a big fat mom-ma tryin' to break___ me. And I love to live so plea-sant - ly,___ live this life of lux - u - ry,___ laz - ing on a sun - ny af - ter - noon,___ in sum-mer - time,___ in sum-mer - time.___

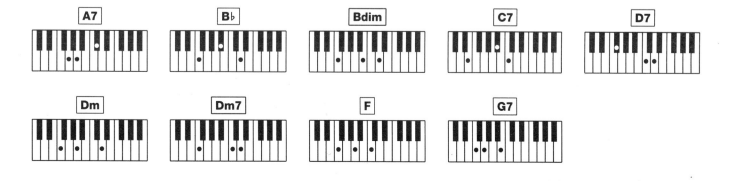

SUNNY SKIES

Words and Music by James Taylor

Suggested Registration: Electric Piano
Rhythm: 8 beat
Tempo: ♩ = 120

Sun-ny skies sleeps in the morn - ing, he does-n't know when to rise,

_ he clo-ses his wea-ry eyes, _ up-on _ the day,

_ look at him yawn - ing, throw-ing his morn-

- ing hours _ a - way, _ he knows how to ease down slow.

Ev-ery-thing is fine in the end, _ and you will be

pleased to know that sun-ny skies has-n't a friend.

Surfin' U.S.A.

Words by Brian Wilson / Music by Chuck Berry

Suggested Registration: Electric Guitar
Rhythm: Rock and Roll
Tempo: ♩ = 152

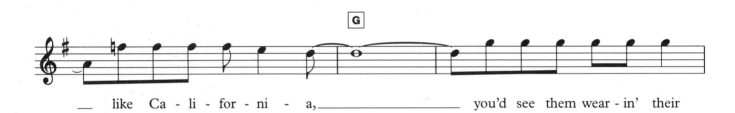

If ev-ery-bo-dy had an o-cean_____ a-cross the U. S. A.,_

_____ then ev-ery-bo-dy'd be surf-in',_____

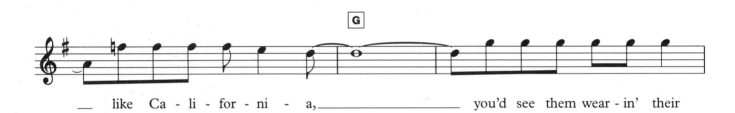

_ like Ca-li-for-ni - a,_____ you'd see them wear-in' their

bag - gies,_____ huar-a-chi san-dals too,_____

_ a bush-y, bush-y blonde hair-do,_____ surf-in' U. S. A.,_

_____ you'll catch 'em surf-in' at Del Mar,_____

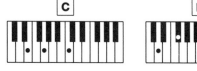  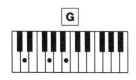

Tequila Sunrise

Words and Music by Don Henley and Glenn Frey

Suggested Registration: Piano
Rhythm: 8 Beat
Tempo: ♩ = 112

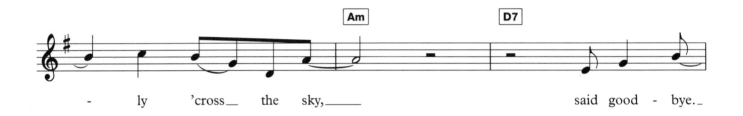

It's an-oth-er te-qui - la sun - rise, start-in' slow-

- ly 'cross the sky,⸺ said good - bye.⸺

He was just a hired⸺ hand,

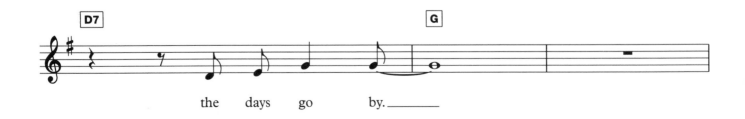

work-in' on the dreams he planned to try,⸺ the days go by.⸺

THAT LUCKY OLD SUN

Words by Haven Gillespie / Music by Beasley Smith

Suggested Registration: Vibraphone
Rhythm: Swing
Tempo: ♩ = 104

The Easy Keyboard Library
also available in this series

Country Songs
including:
Don't It Make My Brown Eye's Blue,
Just When I Needed You Most,
The Rose and Stand By Your Man

Classic Hits Volume 1
including:
All Woman, From A Distance,
I'd Do Anything For Love
(But I Won't Do That) and Show Me Heaven

Classic Hits Volume 2
including:
Don't Go Breaking My Heart,
Heal The World,
My Baby Just Cares For Me and
What A Wonderful World

Showtunes
including:
Anything Goes, Forty-Second Street,
I Remember It Well and
Lullaby Of Broadway

Number One Hits
including:
Congratulations, Moon River,
Stand By Me and Without You

Film Classics
including:
I Will Always Love You, Chariots
Of Fire, Aces High and Mona Lisa

Love Songs Volume 1
including:
Careless Whisper,
The First Time Ever I Saw Your Face,
Saving All My Love For You
and True Love

Love Songs Volume 2
including:
I'll Be There, Love Me Tender,
Where Do I Begin? (Love Story) and
You've Lost That Lovin' Feelin'

Christmas Songs
including:
Another Rock & Roll Christmas,
Frosty The Snowman, Jingle Bells and
Mistletoe And Wine

Soul Classics
including:
Fever, My Girl, (Sittin' On) The Dock
Of The Bay and When A Man Loves
A Woman

TV Themes
including:
Birds Of A Feather, Coronation Street, Last
Of The Summer Wine and Match Of The Day

Big Band Hits
including:
Come Fly With Me, In The Mood,
It's Only A Paper Moon and Secret Love